BY THE AUTHOR

Poetry as Maggie Butt

Quintana Roo (Acumen 2003)

Lipstick (Greenwich Exchange 2007)

I Am The Sphinx (Snakeskin 2008)

petite (Hearing Eye 2010)

Ally Pally Prison Camp (Oversteps Books 2011)

Sancti-Clandestini – Undercover Saints (Ward-Wood 2012)

Degrees of Twilight (The London Magazine Editions 2015)

everlove (The London Magazine Editions 2021)

Edited non-fiction

Story, the Heart of the Matter (Greenwich Exchange 2007)

Novels as Maggie Brookes

The Prisoner's Wife (Penguin Random House 2020)

Acts of Love and War (Penguin Random House 2022)

WISH

WISH

New and Selected Poems

MAGGIE BROOKES-BUTT

Greenwich Exchange
London

Greenwich Exchange, London

First published in Great Britain in 2025
All rights reserved

Wish: New and Selected Poems
Maggie Brookes-Butt © 2025

This book is sold subject to the conditions that it shall not, by way of trade or otherwise, be lent, resold, hired out or otherwise circulated without the publisher's prior consent in any form of binding or cover other than that in which it is published and without a similar condition including this condition being imposed on the subsequent purchaser.

Printed and bound by imprintdigital.com
Cover design by Tim Butt
Cover Art:

Author website: maggiebutt.co.uk
Facebook: Maggie Brookes-Butt
Instagram: Maggie__Brookes

Greenwich Exchange website: www.greenex.co.uk

Cataloguing in Publication Data is available from the British Library

ISBN: 978-1-910996-85-0

To my wonderful family. Everlove.

CONTENTS

Grand: New Poems

Welcome *15*

Murmur *16*

Me *17*

Eyes *18*

Skin *20*

Falling in Love *21*

Nuances of Fear *22*

The Conundrum of Proportion *23*

Angelos *24*

Confounding Time *26*

Degrees of Affection *27*

Infinite Variety *28*

Dizzy *29*

Imagination *30*

Yoga *31*

Remembering *32*

Matryoshka *34*

Realities 35

In Plain Sight *36*

Certainty *37*

This is My Advice to You *38*

from *Lipstick* (2007)

Lipstick *41*

Star-Lit *42*

Nylon Sheets *43*

On My 85th Birthday *44*

Bulbs *45*

Gap Year *46*

Fathering *47*

Royal Vintage *48*

Handkerchief *49*

Love Seeps In *50*

from *petite* (2011)

Luck *53*

Self-Portrait in a Blue Room *54*

I Am As Happy *55*

Pigalle *56*

The Shape of It *57*

What Would I Give *58*

List *59*

This Moment *60*

from *Ally Pally Prison Camp* (2011)

Otto Weiss - Canary Breeder *63*

Killing Time *64*

It's Just *65*

Allotments *66*

from *Sancti Clandestini - Undercover Saints* (2012)

The Patron Saint of Eco-Warriors *69*

The Patron Saint of Ugly Towns *70*

The Patron Saint of Tattooists *71*

from *Degrees of Twillight* (2015)

The Archaeology of Hotel Rooms *75*

Time Travellers *76*

Behind Me *78*

The New Mothers *79*

Go Gentle *80*

Etruscan Cemetery, Orvieto *81*

Risk Assessment *82*

The Working Day Commences *83*

Unfinished *84*

Meltwater *85*

Wish *86*

from *everlove* (2021)

Torn *89*

Toil *90*

Shoes *91*

Flood *92*

Hope-road *94*

Fret *96*

The Children *97*

Last Swim of the Season *98*

March *100*

everlove *101*

Now I Must Be *102*

Dawn Chorus in Amherst *103*

Batting Partnership: 34 Not Out *104*

All About the Light *106*

Acknowledgements

GRAND

New Poems

for Tilly, Etta and any future grandchildren

WELCOME

Welcome to the violet haze of bluebell
woods, to holloways and chalk streams,
sea-silk billowing to the horizon, mist
puddling in fields, spiders' webs etched
with rime, to numberless stars, the smells
of cinnamon buns and rain on concrete;
the voice of the wren and Bob Marley
on a sunny afternoon; the tang of ginger
beer, liquorice and blackcurrant jam;
to our honeyed songs and rocking arms,
our hopeful dreams, fussing and fretting,
laughter, quiet sleep, warm skin, kind
words. Welcome to you: blood of my blood,
heart of my heart, world of my world.

MURMUR

My heart is whispering – this faint back-wash
is slush and suck of waves over shingle,
tumbling the stones which will lie underwater
when storms rage far above their flooded world.

My heart is whispering – a breeze turns
over leaves, its shivery message passes
from branch to branch at the far-off crackle
of forest flames and thudding feet of animals.

But whispers lullaby your sleeping form,
your peaceful unknowing, sharing secrets
of here-and-gone, here-and-gone. Listen
to its echo: love ... love ... love ...

ME

What lightning strike
of insight has told you
the curly-haired girl
in the mirror is 'me?'

   when nobody calls you that
   and everyone else also
   claims to be 'me?'

Rejoice in your
new-found me-ness,
bright as a freshly minted penny

   and if a teen-time comes
   when you long to blend in
   invisible-me, avatar-me,
   do what you need to survive,
   chameleon-me

but guard a bright sliver
of toddler-me somewhere
deep inside, a seed-me, stem-cell-me
so you can unfurl back into yourself
a springtime fern-frond-me

   and if by then I'm far away,
   a misty memory, love that girl
   as fiercely as I do.
   Love me.

EYES

Mine have seen first breaths and lasts,
the beginning and end of everything,

green shoots and heaps of rotting leaves.
They've seen horses pulling coal drays,

milk bottle tops pecked by blue-tits,
peace camps, walls torn down, glass

ceilings cracking, gay weddings,
but children slippered in class, life vests

washed up beside migrant boats, turtles
choked by plastic bags, smoking ruins.

Mine are hooded now, the teal and amber
marbled irises surrounded by crinkled deltas

of skin, but still see clearly thanks to small
acrylic miracles and astonishing dexterity.

Yours are wide and bright, the whites whiter
than paper, almost blue, the irises two shades

of grey, dove grey circled by wet-slate grey.
They can spot the smallest dot of crumb,

bending to retrieve it, or point to the woods
where a squirrel is camouflaged against a trunk.

I can see what's coming, my vision unclouded
by the twin cataracts of helplessness and dismay.

Polar bears claim abandoned villages. Tanks roll
in again. Together we watch the leaves fall.

SKIN

The trees have come back from the dead
each year of my life, and my amazing skin
which keeps out wet, and keeps in body parts,
and sings the touch of yours, has regenerated
eight hundred times, each renewal loosening
just a micron, losing a little of the taut brightness
of yours, like a photocopy of a photocopy,
the definition and colour fading away.

You might inherit my crinkles and sags,
as I did from my mother, age spots like puddles
of cold tea from my grandmother. It may not be
the inheritance you'd choose. I wish I could bequeath
you skin that's armoured like a rhinoceros
or armadillo, against a world where I won't be here
to run to, to bury your face in my chest, to shield
you against the rising waters of that too-imaginable
future. I wrap you in love – stronger than spider-web,
silk, dyneema; tougher than diamonds, kevlar,
tungsten; long-lasting as uranium, thorium, light.

FALLING IN LOVE

Again and again, every time surely the last,
each one with a shock like being knocked down
by a giant wave, bowled over and over in the shallows
gasping for air; and from the first this squeeze
of pain around the heart, longing for one glimpse,
each desert day without sight of the beloved;
'It's Thursday, he might be there, might notice
me'; that time I fell asleep on the school coach
and rested my head on his shoulder, woke,
pretending to still be asleep, aching with the need
to move, aching with the desire never to move;
and now it overwhelms me again, as unfightable
as the first, all-engulfing as meeting the eyes
of our own daughters, submerged and breathless
in the simultaneous joy and fear of losing them;
this secretly longed-for, unexpected gift
your delighted little dance when you see me
at the door, your arms reaching to be picked up
and each time I am drowned again.

NUANCES OF FEAR

Out walking in a village street yesterday I met
a young woman leading a frisky colt who was backing
and shying as if spooked by ghosts. 'It's puddles,'
she explained, 'He's afraid of puddles.' She laughed
but I thought he must be terrified of that rival horse
in his own reflection, and the unfathomable depths.

You are like the colt, not yet knowing what to fear,
so: you do not have to be frightened of hairdryers,
loud noises, wolves under beds, balloons, or people
dressed as Peter Rabbit. Scorpions yes, but spiders,
bees, snakes and sharks not as much as you'd imagine.
Mosquitoes, dogs and humans are deadlier. Not thunder,
but its electric mother, lightning. Avoid dark alleys
and bullies if you can; be wary of strangers, but
then how will you be warmed by their kindness?

I'd love to say don't be scared of looking foolish,
but that takes sixty years to learn. For now leave
fear about the drowning and scorching of your world
to me. I have enough for both of us. When I'm too
voiceless to protest, too old to carry a placard,
I'll hand it to you like a baton or perhaps a fiery
sword, and you can run in my stead. We will defy
the politicians with lies for hair, shout down
fearfulness itself with tongues of flame.

THE CONUNDRUM OF PROPORTION

You try to force your arm into dolly's dress
balance her hat like a pimple on your head,
crush her cardboard-box bed with your giant toddler
body, puzzled by further mysteries of perspective:
big or close; small or far away; the way your feelings
rear up huge as a tidal wave and threaten to drown
the world till reason is a whisper in a hurricane.
Beware adults who tell you to 'keep it in proportion'.
They might also believe that *code red for humanity*
is small and far away.

The UN's Intergovernmental Panel on Climate Change warned in 2021 that the global threat level posed by climate change was 'a code red for humanity'.

ANGELOS

In a world where the loudest sounds were shouting,
dog-bark, birdsong, the clatter of horses' hooves

on cobbled streets, blacksmiths' hammer blows
or thunder claps – when angels spoke, their voices

reverberated and even kings might stop and listen
as they proclaimed mysteries like peace and love,

unknown to warlike humankind; but now their songs
are lost in the noise, carried away like thistledown

on the wind, while their name has shape-shifted
down centuries, *malakh* to *angelos*, Hebrew to Greek,

messengers transmuted into angels who now burn
with incandescent fury. They've delivered tidings

and warnings over and over, with data and science,
but most people simply shrug and bat them away.

So they desperately resort to glueing themselves
to motorways, hurling orange paint on gardens,

the children dancing behind Greta out of school,
because only they tuned in and turned their heads,

watching the flames and ice-melt, recognising
the unmistakeable colour and tangy flavour of truth,

still having a quiet place inside them to hear.
Breathe my darling. Learn to listen.

CONFOUNDING TIME

We say, 'not now', 'in a minute',
'later', 'maybe tomorrow' but how
can you dream there will be another
now, brimming with delight
and sorrow, bright as a morning,
temporary as the dew on the hostas?

Hold my hand and we'll wander down
our together-years, though yours fan out
ahead like a country road disappearing
over a hill, while mine might stop
at the next stile or that tree on the rise.

I have too little left to save the world
for you, but see the Nerine – when her
leaves are wrinkled and wilted, drooping
over the edge of the pot like something
you should throw on the compost, wait ...
that's when she pushes up green spears,
bladed and pointed, battle-ready, which open
into a blaze of pink stars and light
the autumn days right through to winter.

DEGREES OF AFFECTION

Remind yourself in years to come
you have been loved like this: more
fiercely than a tiger cub, more softly
than a moth-wing. Not just enough
to dry between each toe, but that I
stop my work ten times a day to feed
on images of you; would suffer
in your stead if you were sick or hurt,
with gladness in my heart, retching,
writhing, shivering, burning to save
you. If a girder fell towards your pram,
I would instantly throw my body over
yours. I'd change the world to smooth
just one step of your path. I am brave
in your defence, furious in your name.
Never settle for less.

INFINITE VARIETY

This a common corn flag, known in America
as whistling jack, and this a Vietnamese pot bellied
pig, though it looks nothing like the pink porker
in your toy farmyard. Dogs can be hand-sized
or big as ponies. They all say woof. Or not.

I can show you ants in the kitchen and clothes moths
in the bedroom, but I'm unlikely to find a beetle
as they live largely in memory. My mum was terrified
of them: stag; chafer; death-watch; devil's coach horse;
cardinal; sexton; in the days when a short drive
would end with a windscreen of squashed bugs.

Though your lips have barely learned to form 'baaa'
and 'moo' you can identify elephant, tiger, giraffe,
run to collect them from your wooden ark, recognise
the strange whinnying sound a panda makes
when calling for a mate, and the unfathomable misery
of whale song, as if they see into the future.

You cock your head to listen to recordings of blackbird,
goldfinch and wren, though will never hear
the pagan reed-warbler; least vermillion flycatcher;
aptly named Gerygone, or the hundreds
of others hunting in vain for an ark.

And this is an oak tree, which is home
to 2,300 species. Wrap your arms around it.
There is only one of you. Do what you can.

DIZZY

I remember doing that – twirling round
        and round in circles until the whole world
swooped and soared like a chair-o-plane
        ride, and never was giddiness such a thrill
again, certainly not when too much vodka
        made the room spin half the night, or
a dodgy heart sent light-headed warnings
        of its troubles. I remember at ballet-class
being taught to jerk my head around while
        pirouetting to remain upright, though whirling
dervishes don't do that, revolving on prayer alone,
        and I've always wondered how we balance
on this circling planet without staggering
        and reeling. You collapse in dizzy-giggles
and I think never was woozy-wobbliness
        such a joy again – except perhaps the
vertiginous delight of loving you.

IMAGINATION

has been my blessing and my curse, transporting
me from grief and loneliness but galloping away
through terrifying nights like horses bolting
with a carriage, living though horrors and dreads
which recede with the dawn, and rarely come to pass.

This I have handed on to you. Already I say
'let's go to the park' and you sweep your chubby arm
around the living room, 'this park' you say, hurling
cushions on the floor, 'this lake', 'this slide', 'this cafe',
as the room transforms itself to zoo and swimming pool,
transports us to summer and Christmas. All manner
of forest animals knock on our curtained den for shelter
from the storm or sometimes big bad wolves prowl
outside and we keep still, until I order them away.

But now a worse fear rises up to grip me as I read
of microplastics, picture them travelling around
your body, threads and beads rivered in your blood
jostling with corpuscles and cells, breathed down
into your clean pink lungs, nestling in the deep ends
of branching alveoli, like the water bottles, buckets,
carrier bags and debris sloshing round our oceans,
even in Antarctica, clogging the beaches, tidal
far into your future, a monster I can't lay to rest.

YOGA

For you, with your toddler bendiness,
the squat is a natural, easy position
while I hurt-strain, and think of miners
crouched outside their front doors
on terraced streets, contorted every day
by the cramped conditions of their work
until the body adjusted and it became
normal, like living without daylight
and breathing dust, just as we inhale
fumes without a second's hesitation.

Forget all that, quiet my whirring brain,
show me how to bow to the animals,
down-dog and cat-cow, rear up together
like cobras, soar into eagles or graceful
cranes flying. Steady each other. My balance
is better than yours for now, though not
my equilibrium. Let us look backwards
between our legs, marvel at the topsy-turvy
world and lie side by side, gripping our toes
while I learn from you how to be happy baby.

REMEMBERING

You are already laying down memories:
fine sand, brightly coloured as Alum bay,
compressing into firm layers of bedrock.

Here are the days we went to the zoo;
the afternoon we spent in the paddling pool
till our fingers crinkled; the picture on the wall

which held story after story about walking
through the woods; conjuring cardboard
box tunnels, slides, boats, cars and castles.

They will all get stamped down and overlaid
by school and friends and your own concerns.
You may not remember me at all. I was eleven

when my nana died and my memories of her
are wisps of smoke. Or perhaps I'll be very old
and crazy, infuriatingly repeating non-sequiturs,

my memories and thoughts eroded, as runnels
carry them away and dig deep gullies into my mind,
leaching away my words faster than you assemble

yours, until you can't excavate the woman
who threaded in and out the dusty bluebells
and showed you how to hopscotch. Don't be sad

if you can't unearth the long cuddles, the books we read together, the cafés and farms and shops we ran, the seeds we sowed. They are still there

somewhere, like treasure resting in the earth for detectorists to find, or Roman roads laying the firm foundations for all you will build.

MATRYOSHKA

'More' you say, 'more' as I twist open
each to reveal its nesting daughter,
delight spiralling till we reach
the baby, smelling sweetly of linden wood
and swaddled: 'tiny', 'tiny'. But not as small
or astonishing as the fact that when I carried
your mummy curled inside my womb,
she already had in her ovaries the egg
which would be you, complete with
your mother's eyes, our hair, determination,
love of books, three generations folded
inside each other, miraculous, tiny, tiny, tiny.

REALITIES

You wouldn't be the slightest bit perturbed if dogs
and cats began to chat in French, or giraffes rode unicycles
and pandas drove fire engines or a witch swooped down
on her broomstick, parked on the lawn and invited you
to hop up and take a ride. All these things you have seen
in books and believe, because your well of trust is bottomless.

How much more of a shock it will be
to discover the truths of acne and the hidden grind
of period pains and unrequited love; of poky flats
in squalid streets with bad smells on the stairs;
of tube trains crammed with people on their way
to mind-numbing jobs with colleagues they despise.

But this is not the worst. The whine of chainsaws
plagues the forests, while glaciers silently drip. Missiles
land on another hospital, another school. And the people
we love go away and we never see them again, though
we never stop loving them. Or does that torrent of grief
when we leave mean that somehow you already know?

Let's not go there today. Better by far to hold my hand
and look for bears in the woods, mermaids diving
from the rocks, Father Christmas landing on the roof,
dance the hokey-cokey and sing 'that's what it's all about.'

IN PLAIN SIGHT

Although your legs stick out under the sofa,
we say, 'Oh no! We've lost her!' and ask 'Is she
in the toy box or behind the door, or in the fridge?'
ignoring your delighted giggles, and we feign
astonishment when you pop out, for we are practised
at not noticing. The emperor's new clothes are
everywhere. We didn't see the world getting hotter,
the rich getting richer, seas bobbing with plastic,
kindness ebbing like water through sand – it all
just jumped out on us. We were busy looking
behind curtains and under cushions for a better world.

CERTAINTY

Not quite twelve months in this world, your feet
so putty-soft they hardly know which part to connect
with the earth, legs not yet bearing your own weight
without stage-drunk lurches, you have discovered
you can pull yourself upright and crab-walk, hand
over hand, sidestepping the length of the sofa
which was surely placed there for your convenience,
and when this support runs out, you thrust one arm
into the air, not looking up, expecting an adult grasp,
and your certainty that another hand will always
be there to clasp threatens to break my heart;
but once you've connected with it, as you knew
you would, your other hand shoots up and grips
hold so you can twist into a forward march
knees raised like a comic soldier, almost swinging
between the arms of the bent-over grown-up,
laughing with delight at all the possibilities.

THIS IS MY ADVICE TO YOU

Grasp happiness with both hands.
When it wriggles and shape-shifts,
becomes a snake, a bear, a fish
wrap your arms tight around it
hug it to your chest. Don't let go.

from
Lipstick (2007)

LIPSTICK

In war time women turn to red
swivel-up scarlet and carmine
not in solidarity with spilt blood
but as a badge of beating hearts.

This crimson is the shade of poets
silenced for speaking against torture,
this vermilion is art
surviving solitary confinement,

this cerise defies the falling bombs
the snipers taking aim at bread-queues,
this ruby's the resilience of girls
who tango in the pale-lipped face of death.

War photographer, Jenny Matthews, noticed that in Bosnia and Afghanistan women favoured bright red lipstick. A 1940s Max Factor catalogue confirmed the same was true during the Second World War.

STAR-LIT

Laughing home barefoot from the disco
star-lit, care-free, safe within the pack
high heels dangling from our hands like bracelets,
cold pavements salve dance-blistered toes,
the pulse of living sings along our blood.
We are reflected in dark High Street windows
so the night is full of us, our youth.
The cars are few, our voices own the air,
and you three boys stride out, long-limbed,
the world laid out before you for the taking,
throw back your heads, cry to the moon,
We are gods!
And I look
and you are.

NYLON SHEETS

This was the future come to pass
test-tube fibres, grown by science

housekeeping purses flew wide
as mouths of hungry baby birds

two pairs for each bed (one in the wash)
Buy British, dream smug in Bri-nylon

bedtime flashed and sparked in pink and mauve
designed by hippies on a psychedelic trip

thus swinging sixties cured the washday blues
no more heaving sodden cotton sheets

between the steamy twin-tub drums
these flew like fledglings, chirruping

replaced the sombre sails along the washing line
with gaudy parakeets, Carnaby Street carnival

dry in a trice and best of all, no ironing
(faint smell of charred bras carried on the wind.)

How did our mothers spend that newly minted time
which made it worth the sweaty, suffocating sleep

the slippery touch, the catching on rough heels
a generation rising charged with static?

ON MY 85TH BIRTHDAY

For breakfast there will be chocolate,
heaped and glossy like a race-horse,
sweating with saturated fat.

And I will devour it,
cramming in the melting mouthfuls
coating my fingers and my face.

In the morning I'll ride a motorbike
black leathers and no helmet
white hair streaming loose, a challenge.

For lunch there will be crispy bacon
in white bread, with butter,
mouthwatering aroma of defiance.

After my nap in the bed-shop window;
I will invite my doctor in for scones,
and lick thick clotted cream along the knife.

And in the sunset
I will ascend to heaven in a glider
singing in the eerie silence.

The next day I'll dance barefoot in the rain
or take up smoking (inhaling deeply)
or sub-aqua diving,
or run with scissors
if I choose.

BULBS
for Amy

I ask you – how the hibernating bulb
knows when to jerk awake?
Pinioned in the ice-dark earth
perpetual night of wet and cold.
How does it know the time has come
to push the bleached blind maggoty shoot
out into the stone-frost dirt
on cue to flower on April 23rd?

I dare you – take a bulb and strip away
its glossy, coppery paper shell
the onion-like white folds on folds
and show me where it keeps the clock
or microchip which tells it when to start
so it will flower to the day with its companions
however chill and damp the spring.
One laggard never oversleeps and pops up in September.

I defy you – take the spiralling DNA of me
the pumping, wooshing ventricles,
the zing-charged porridge in my head,
and show me where I keep the love for you
that will outlast my life.

GAP YEAR

(iv) Demeter
When you tuck your daughter on the train
and watch her wan face slide into the night
and you are left upon the platform
with your tears, so small within your skin,
shrunk to a whisper as love pulls away;
you turn towards the tube's wide mouth
descending to the hot rebreathing air,
knowing how simple it would be
to ride the escalator into Hades' flames
if you had just a whisker of a chance
to bring her back with you.

(v) Parting
No wonder the heart gives out in the end
throws up its hands and cries surrender
when it is stretched so many times in parting
like over-washed elastic.

FATHERING

Because I could not bear to let you go
my body found a way to bring you back.

Part-dormant genes pushed out a root
and half of me took flower.

My jowls drop just a feather's breadth
until your jaw-line smiles back from the mirror.

I swim the strokes you longed
and my slow breathing meets with yours.

You use my eyes to note the detail of the world
your calmness soothes my path like honey.

Because I could not bear to let you go
my body found a way to bring you back.

ROYAL VINTAGE

A court of princes froths from the school gate
each one is crowned, lord of delight,
in gold card, glitter gems, foil sapphires
clear as eyes. Fresh from nativity and tight
with cake and games and lemonade
they glow the street's too-early night
bubbling, fermented, sun-drenched crop
fizz towards Christmas, bauble-bright.

The hand-held adults, wholly in their thrall
will store this vintage in the cellars of the mind
to uncork radiance when the prince is tall.

HANDKERCHIEF

I drink the slope of fields
of stone walled cottages
small lambs, wired for bounce,
and wish I could fold up the countryside
and pocket it, to open on a sordid
city dawn, like a fresh linen handkerchief.

LOVE SEEPS IN

Love seeps in and fills me up
as water overruns a sinking ship,
snaking down corridors
coating them with silver,
bubbling through cracks and crevices
thundering up staircases,
claiming everything.

from
petite (2011)

LUCK

Do you believe in luck?
That second's tick, rice-paper thin
which steps your step in step
with one who will be all in all to you;
that shimmer in the air which separates
you from the crashing car, the flying glass,
the straying bullet, crumpled metal,
blood and pain; the sigh of prayer
which wafts the virus past your head
and off into the night?

SELF-PORTRAIT IN BLUE ROOM
Perranporth

Part room, part sky, high in a house
just anchored to the world, straining
like a kite tugging at its string;
the curve of ceiling, curve of roof,
lifting off into a cobalt sky; a lark-wing
room to ride the summer thermals,
soar and swoop in cornflower light
reflected from sea to wedgwood walls;
and the days ahead in a mermaid room
for growing gills and never surfacing
to breathe; and me in the room, spun out
from the world in the blue of the light
and the seagull cries and the bark
of a dog and the crisp of the air;
free-wheeling down a country hill,
feet off the pedals, wild into the wind.

I AM AS HAPPY

as a man whose house, juddered
in a landslide, comes to rest

just where he'd always hoped to live
overlooking the sweep of bay.

Stepping up the path and opening
his front door, he finds vibration

has loosed a bag of diamonds
hidden in the rafters, which now lie

winking at him, all over the floor.

PIGALLE
for Katie

This rue is where my daughter plans to live:
a tattoo artist yells across the street
where old drunks sun their leathered chests and give
her leering looks; the teenage whores entreat
each passing tourist; dealers thrive like weeds;
a corner bar boasts cross-dress cabaret;
the scent of urine rises; heat forms beads
of sweat – a spring Parisian bouquet.

But strangers clink their glasses in the park
and she will climb five flights of champagne night
where rooftops of Montmartre after dark
gleam with reflected gold and ruby light,
throw wide the shutters, sip the air's rich wine,
intoxicated, think, 'All this is mine.'

THE SHAPE OF IT
for Tim

two
at first
entwined
then billowing
out, sails brimmed
with wind, belly with
movement, house with noise
and muddle, hours crammed
with loud and rush and full,
until doors start to close
peace settles and
I see that it will
narrow down
at last to
just we
two

WHAT WOULD I GIVE

to hear again, beyond my leaden limbs,
their voices calling from the wakeful world,
the sounds which wash like closing waters – skim
above my head, my body's foetal furl,
my eyelids' weight – and lap me far adrift
in dreams? So snuggly-warm and unaware
it would be cruel spite to make me lift
my head, to shake and haul myself upstairs.

Then I imagine, one more time, I feel
the strength of arms which gather me aloft,
still more asleep than not, safe in the steal
and rhythm of their steps, until the soft
of pillowed kiss. However long I live,
to feel that one more time, what would I give?

LIST

Just a sec, I know they're here somewhere,
if you'd stop rushing me I'd find them.
Perhaps I might have packed them in a case,
or wrapped brown paper, tied with string.
They might be in the loft or shed, or, ah! Look now –
my crumpled list of Great Good Things to spend
a life upon. And so they must be here ...
Under the bed? Or slipped between the pages of a book,
the minutes of a day? Re-check the list. Oh dear.
No ticks. I lost the list and have been busy with
I don't know what. But there's still time. Give me
the list, I'll start today. What do you mean?
Right now? No time to get my coat? ...

THIS MOMENT

Sunlight through leaves throws dappled shadows on the wall;
the telephone sighs to rest in its cradle, shifts to get comfortable;
fish defrosts on the work-top, drips pensively onto the plate;
the cat turns, skirts an unseen obstacle, starts to wash its ears;
I call a rushed good-bye while thinking of something else:
the un-hung washing, un-paid bill, un-lived dream,
headlights which raked the ceiling of my childhood room.

from
Ally Pally Prison Camp (2011)

During the first world war more than 3,000 'enemy aliens' were interred at a 'concentration camp' at Alexandra Palace in North London. The park was surrounded by belts of barbed wire, with watchtowers and 'Tommies with fixed bayonets' patrolling between the wires. The 3,000 civilian prisoners at Ally Pally had English wives and children, and many owned businesses in Britain. Many had left Germany as children themselves, or had been born in England, and spoke no German. Only their passports made them 'enemy aliens.' In their own words, in paintings and in poems, this is their story.

OTTO WEISS - CANARY BREEDER

I line up in the damping drizzle
under the stares of soldiers,

disgruntled at their back-seat task,
itching to use the friendly bayonet,

feeling through our feet the rumble
of the guns in France, a bass-line

to the songs of birds I name first
in the names my mother taught,

stop guiltily as if the soldiers hear
my thoughts, correct myself: Robin,

Thrush and Wren; wonder who fed
my liebling birds today, lifted covers

from their wicker cages, let their notes
fly out into the room above the shop

as if I almost hear them, gladdening
the morning, pure as water.

The rain comes heavier, trickles
down the back of my neck. The birds

one by one, fall silent.

KILLING TIME

Who would have guessed its death would be as loud?
That sawing, filing, hammering would mark
time's murder, its deafening butchery?

That minutes must be bayoneted one by one
with clamour, in workshops and at bed-sides
carving, beating, pounding, all the daylight hours?

We longed for a quick end to days and weeks
of grievous separation, swift as pistol shot
or running through with a clean blade,

but every second must be lured, distracted
filled with furious activity before it breathes
its last, bubbling with reluctant blood.

Each morning, after fitful sleep, a new day
to be tortured, poisoned, shaken until its teeth
chatter in its head, driven mad with ceaseless noise.

IT'S JUST

It's just a cold dear.
We all have colds.
the laundry flutters with our handkerchiefs
flags of surrender.

It's just a cough dear.
We all have coughs.
A thousand hacking men who bark
all night, keeping sleep at bay.

Do I look thin dear?
We all look thin.
The fish is sometimes rotten
and it twists within our guts.

It's just a life dear.
We all have lives.
Some spill them in the trenches
others in a cage.

It's just a war dear.
We all have war.

ALLOTMENTS

We are peasants, toiling in a book of hours,
four hundred serfs with meagre strips of land
backs bent to digging, weeding, harvesting,
hearts slowed to medieval grace, at last a flowering
acceptance that days will stretch to seasons
whether we rage against our fate, or not.

We count in older ways, a seed for each imprisoned
man; hold conversations about rain and soil,
varieties – the early or the late, a Dutch hoe
or an English; covet seeds like gold in twists
of paper; our cuttings hoarded, traded, swapped;
the land which hates us, blooming in our hands.

We have a purpose now, the slop-free carrying
of cans of water, tucking in the seedlings
watching over them like children. We grow gifts
of vegetables or flowers to give on visit day,
the taste of fresh picked peas, the currency of crops,
the bud and root of unexpected peace.

from
Sancti Clandestini
– Undercover Saints (2012)

There are official patron saints of wax-melters, truss makers, lumberjacks, Florentine cheese makers and disappointing children. This book proposes some alternative, imaginary saints, including the patron saints of liars, looters, compulsive hoarders, and old dogs.

THE PATRON SAINT OF ECO-WARRIORS

She watches us who fiddle while earth burns,
wonders why we do not lie awake
confronting the enormity, but hope
some scientists will clever us out
of trouble, paddle our raft to safety.

She looks around for samurai,
and once she touches them, they burn
like convent girls, ablaze to truth
revealed to just the chosen few, zealous
as converts, as if their fingers
have been jammed into electric
sockets, and purpose blazes in their heads.

Thus branded, they go forth to save
the tiger, turn algae into fuel, build cars
to run on water, sail rainbow ships,
lie in front of bulldozers, wave
goodbye to families to live in tents
or trees, driven, pure as waterfalls.

She scorns the saintly micro-miracles –
stigmata, healing, water into wine.
Her sights are high: if she can pull it off
her warriors will clinch the miracle
to end all miracles, for they will save the earth.

THE PATRON SAINT OF UGLY TOWNS

You've been to towns like this: shabby
as an old tramp, unwashed and moth-eaten,
shambling along from day to day; ringed
by black mountains, glowering against
the sun; paint peeling from the buildings
exposing plaster like old sores; a market
thronged with tired people in cheap shoes,
stalls heaped with out-size knickers, floral
aprons, itchy socks; a town where work
is history, mines closed, a slag heap
like their self-respect, where even stubby
trees refuse to grow, grass fails to root.
Out in fields the sunflowers bow their heavy
heads like congregations at a funeral,
listening to their doom, counting the hours.

My candles gutter in a grimy church
where mildew blooms on leaky walls,
and you might think my task as hopeless
as world peace. But watch me fly and brush
a feathered wing tip here or there:
a crow drops next year's sunflower seeds,
the gangly boy pulls down his cuffs and
slicks his hair for his first heart-race date,
a tabby cat twines round the widow's legs,
the pregnant woman feels first fluttering kicks.
Watch me fly, and see love shudder into life.

THE PATRON SAINT OF TATTOOISTS

I choose the ripples of your living flesh –
my paintings breathe, sweat, shimmer, soak the sun
not trapped in gloomy halls, or fixed on plaster
in the cold apse of a church. Oh yes, they'd last,
but not know anything of love: that certainty
of names within a heart; the scar which shows
where love once was (the name erased, though memory
still breathes); the only choice when boys go off to war,
(no call for death's heads, anchors, lips and roses then)
he creeps in, sheepish, says the one word, *Mum*.
I give him that. From skin to skin he takes her
to his grave, as she goes down with him.

from
Degrees of Twilight (2015)

THE ARCHAEOLOGY OF HOTEL ROOMS

It's almost always August in hotels,
and always present tense. Owned and occupied,
without past or future; our breath fills its space.
Layers fine as millefeuille, sweet with sugar dust,
pot-shards and fragments, photo-bright.

The surface is Moroccan silk, harem-scarlet
shot with sunset gold, the hum of air-conditioning,
comforting as money. Storks clack like football rattles
on the roof – sign of good luck, as if I didn't
smell the deep spice of it – saffron, turmeric, paprika.

Peel back years like faded floral wallpaper,
good fortune pasted on good fortune.
Find a wide room for families, small dormitory
of watchfulness, blue with Italian light;
detail of sleeping faces, fine as an old master.

Down to a Paris room where flowerprint grew over
walls and ceiling, door-back, curtains, counterpane.
A room with no way out, where none was wanted;
this space held everything there was, hot-house
of universe and time, love's here and now.

Sift softly, blow those grains, flick squirrel brush,
back to the first, foreign with the unknown smell
of garlic, which loitered like a stranger on the stairs.
Baroque figures winked down on me in bolstered bed
cloaks flying, into the unknown summers.

TIME TRAVELLERS

The sick are well, dead smiling, old are young,
framed photos bloom on windowsills and walls,
I am a baby, arms aloft to be picked up,
time zig-zags like a running man avoiding bullets.

Framed photos bloom on windowsills and walls
I am veiled bride, gowned graduate, new mum,
time zig-zags like a running man avoiding bullets,
listen to the echoes of our laughter.

I am veiled bride, gowned graduate, new mum,
we are in Venice with our grown-up daughters,
listen to the echoes of our laughter.
I am a girl, in cotton frock with poodle-print,

We are in Venice with our grown-up daughters,
three straw-haired nieces squint into the sun,
I am a girl, in cotton frock with poodle-print.
Faces unwrinkle, hair turns luxuriant and brown,

three straw-haired nieces squint into the sun,
a bunch of snowdrops, roses, autumn leaves.
Faces unwrinkle, hair turns luxuriant and brown,
he's in a de-mob suit, leaving the war behind,

a bunch of snowdrops, roses, autumn leaves.
Mum is a red-cross nurse, dad like a movie star
he's in a de-mob suit, leaving the war behind
futures latent as a roll of undeveloped film.

Mum is a red-cross nurse, dad like a movie star
I am a baby, arms aloft to be picked up
futures latent as a roll of undeveloped film,
the sick are well, dead smiling, old are young.

BEHIND ME

Here I am again, fumbling
to dress in the dark and cold,
reluctant as a dormouse from its nest,
off to work before the roads
are clogged with cars. Weary.

But today, I glimpse them
from the corner of my eye,
my grandmothers and all
my great-grandmothers,
up before dawn, shawls
pulled around their shoulders,
off to mills and factories
and scrubbing other people's
floors. Their strength
reinforces my bones.

We fill the kettle, glance
at the last star, fierce
in an indigo sky; we fuel
ourselves with jam and tea;
we brush our hair, arrange
our public face and pull
the front door closed, quietly,
not to wake the family.

We step into another day
where the sky lightens.

THE NEW MOTHERS

We sat and cried that third day, concrete-breasted
torn and stitched. We cried for love which opens
and closes like a fist, flooding caves within the heart.

*(Our tears a free-fall leap of waterfall from jungle cliff,
the fury of a summer storm, dashing down petals,
a bone-cold drenching in rivulets along the scalp.)*

We cried relief to find ourselves and you alive, breathing
past the pain. We cried for those before, mothers
in mossy churchyards, or coffins shoe-box small.

*(Our tears the steady pour of winter down a drain-pipe,
the leak of roof to overflowing buckets, bowls and dishes,
the ceaseless night-long drip of worn-out-washer tap.)*

We cried for all the falls we can't womb you against:
the bully teachers, failures, phone calls in the night
beyond our arms. We paid up-front in tears.

GO GENTLE
In argument with Dylan Thomas

Why not go gentle into that good night
like drifting into sleep from sun-soaked day,
remembering the brightness of the light?

Weary of gross indignities, take flight,
wave off the drugs, dementia, slow decay,
why not go gentle into that good night?

Good housewives, who have polished fiercely bright
both floors and faces, earned this holiday
remembering the brightness of the light.

Wild women who could drink and dance all night
flop down and kick your achy shoes away,
why not go gentle into that good night?

Grave women, who face death with failing sight
let memory fling you back from this cold clay
remembering the brightness of the light.

And you my mother, here on this sad height,
dive cleanly from your tower of fear, I pray.
Why not go gentle into that good night,
remembering the brightness of the light?

ETRUSCAN CEMETERY, ORVIETO

Neat rows of tombs, unsealed and long defiled
gape wide as slack-jawed skulls, while tides of green
have lapped into their rocky coves, a wash
of moss and fern and ivy in their humid hearts.

Town of the dead, with swept, paved streets;
a downward flight of steps behind each door.
Town of the loved, of houses built to last
a thousand years, to withstand earthquake,

war and the slow mounding up of earth.
Town of gods long since eclipsed, snuffed out.
Town of echoes and a hush of leaves,
a whirr of wings, a bird's lament, the twitch

of lizard in dry grass, the ghosts who ask,
*What did you do with my love? I laid her here
with oil and spice. I built a home and carved
her name over the door.* A town of eyes

at my back, whispering and whispering,
*Where has my love gone? Where
has she gone?* Overhead the careless
blue, and underfoot the stone-heart earth.

RISK ASSESSMENT

Dress up your superstitions with new names,
the future is a cliff edge in the dark.
Seem scientific, plan insurance claims,
dress up your superstitions with new names,
cast runes, deal tarot, hear the stars' refrain.
However much you plan, the truth is stark,
dress up your superstitions with new names,
the future is a cliff edge in the dark.

THE WORKING DAY COMMENCES

I wake early in the paddock with the sleeping
lions. A muscle twitches under a tawny flank.
A tufted tail flicks at a fly. The sun rises.
I turn to creep back into dreams but a heavy head
lifts and yawns, and then another, shaking
a sleepy mane. And one by one they struggle
to their feet, their amber eyes fixed on me,
and at my back a silent fence rises between me
and the open country of sleep. The lions advance
with their deliberate paws and their ready teeth.

UNFINISHED

Six hundred years since Michelangelo
started to chip away a slave, straining
for freedom, muscles bulging on torso
and arm, head twisted, tugging for liberty.
Then, called to Rome, abandoned him
half woken, stuck as a fly in amber,
fighting to release himself from marble.

In the next gallery, a muted fresco,
Christ in his rough-hewn tomb, struggling
to sit up, head and shoulders slumped
in pain, weighed down with the world's
suffering, wounds and bruises throbbing,
half-alive and longing for that untroubled,
numbing sleep he has surrendered.

The slave interred in marble doesn't hear
those warning tears of grief and separation.
He chooses life, each drop of agony and joy:
to yawn his yet unfinished yawn, stretch like a cat,
flex his rigid muscles; feel his skin against
another's, taste her mouth; to run until his heart
bangs in his chest, lungs burn; feel it all.

Accademia Gallery, Firenze
'The Awakening Slave' Michelangelo Buonarroti
'Christ As The Man of Sorrows' Andrea del Sarto.

MELTWATER

My time is coming, smell it on the wind
watch raindrops winnowing down glass

touch ice-cube to your lips and tongue
feel the cool chemistry of meltwater

see me submerge fields and swallow crops
spill out of wells to infiltrate your graves

raising the dead; firm ground will swamp
to ooze and squelch and slip, mud-symphony

hear gurgles, trickles, runnels in your sleep
reach for the drifting flotsam of your dreams

sweep river-sludge and sewage from the rug
swell my boundaries with your salt tears;

heave seas, wide breaths to rear up hills
waves come to claim their lost inheritance

listen to the future: rain-rocked, lake-like
nothing divides the waters from the waters.

WISH

in the wheel of the stars
and the mow of the hay
in the blaze of amaze
at the birth of the day

in the whirr on the wire
and the scorch of the sun
in the warm and the storm
and the world on the run

in the roil and the broil
of the clouds' heaving heap
in the indigo dusk
and the drifting to sleep

in the flap of a wing
or the bat of an eye
the slowness of Sunday
years scampering by

in the damp of the drizzle
the warmth of a glove
let there ever be you
let there ever be love

from
everlove (2021)

This sequence was inspired by the work of American painter Mary Behrens in her series of distorted and reassembled photographs of refugees called *Run*.

TORN

someone
someone took your life
your life and tore it down the middle
down the middle then crossways into smaller
smaller pieces as if it was a letter
a letter from an unfaithful lover
pieces flying to the wind.

So now you know that the gods, the fates
the fates, the gods
care less for you than a scrap of paper
a scrap of paper.

And though you run about
run about and catch them all
all blowing and raining about you
like ticker-tape
tickertape
you can't see how
how you could begin
begin to stick them together
stick them together
to make a life again.

So you tuck them carefully
carefully into your pocket and walk
and walk
and walk.

TOIL

You used to work once.
In a bank perhaps, a school,
or on a building site.
Your work had name and status
in which you dressed every morning.
I am a carpenter, you'd say,
a mathematician, a housewife,
an HR consultant.

Now your work is laying a bedsheet
on the floor, heaping it with the objects
you can't bear to leave behind:
family photographs; letters; addresses;
a candle-holder your daughter made;
your favourite book; a change of clothes;
if you are lucky, some money
and jewellery, stuffed into a sock;
your phone; food which won't moulder.
Your job is to tie this sheet
corner to corner, and carry it.
Your new work has a name too:
the one who seeks refuge
and is reviled.
But you clothe yourself in it
because you have no other.

SHOES

I think about shoes.
Just that.

If I had to choose just one pair
to yank on quick
to leave right now
to run from the rubble
which was my home
to who knows where
no time to think
I'd grab the comfiest
but they are houseshoes
townshoes
calling-on-friends shoes
with soles I can already feel
uneven pavement through
and they may be starting to leak.

How far would I have to walk?
How long would they need to last?

FLOOD

its end shall come with a flood,
and to the end there shall be war

in great haste, the people gather up their bundles
and the rain descended, and the floods came,
and the winds blew
and beat upon that house, and it fell, and great was the fall of it

the people gather their children to their breast
all the fountains of the great deep burst forth

the rivers burst their banks and the bridges wash away
a tempest of hail, a destroying storm,
a flood of mighty waters overflowing

flash-floods rush down the wadis, carrying all before them
the floods have lifted up their voice;
the floods lift up their roaring waves

the people wade through the swirling waters
the stormy wind lifts up the waves of the sea

they wade through the thigh-deep, waist-deep, surging flood
I sink in deep mire, where there is no foothold;
I am come into deep waters, where the floods overflow me

the children cling to their parents;
the parents cling to their children
for the waves of death encompassed me,

the torrents of destruction assailed me;
the sorrows of hell compassed me about

the people grip onto each other, slipping and sliding
you sweep them away as with a flood;
they are like a dream

Quotes from The Bible

HOPE-ROAD

long straight dustroad
young father pram-pushes
young mother handholds small child
wool stockings but no shoes
woman breastfeeds under tarpaulin
tent sold for food
child has deepcrease between eyes
this is America

girl says
road should oughter go someplace better'n where you are

corpse in church porch
man slumped headholds
woman lugs pail
other-arm thrown out
just balancing
men suit-and-hatted curl on sidewalk
sleep without pillows
this is America

girl says
that's the reason for a road

woman handclasps forehead
pulls up lips into rictus
holdsback howl
stoop labour in fields
bent hairpin-backs
four legged beasts
this is America

girl says
there's hope in a road, right?

long straight dustroad
climbs out-of-Egypt
towards promisedland

Inspired by the photographs of Dorothea Lange.
Quotes from a girl she photographed.

FRET

What did you lie awake in the night
worrying about, before?
Was it the highsky, deepsea matters:
how best to live your life, how
to walk lightly on this trembling earth?

Or did you only have space in the crush
and rush of days to worry about
what the doctor told your father,
why the teacher bullies your child,
how to evade the anger of your boss,
whether someone still loves you,
if it's safe to drive on so little sleep?

And were those frets shoved aside
like somebody elbowing their way
through the marketplace of your life
by how to put food in your son's bowl,
when the bombs will fall again,
whether your daughter is still alive?

And now. What do you worry about
when all the worst is true?

THE CHILDREN

have folded their banners and gone back to school
because there is no plastic clogging the oceans
or CO_2 belching into the skies. All the forest fires
are quenched and the glaciers frozen solid.

They daydream out of classroom windows, watch
a fly crawl up the pane in the slow afternoon
because all endangered animals are breeding
and trees are flowering in the deserts.

They giggle and jostle in the playground
because there are no gangs with knives,
no teenagers weeping over the bodies of their mates,
no internet bullies, and trolls are just in fairytales.

They wander home to eat their favourite tea
with no families queuing at foodbanks,
no refugees fleeing war and famine, no
posturing politicians squaring up to each other.

They slip under duvets and drift into untroubled sleep
knowing tomorrow will be another uneventful day
lush with quietness, opening like a gift.

LAST SWIM OF THE SEASON

The freezelick of waves ices my toes, instanumbs
    calves, thighs, stomach, so there's a minim
of a moment when I swingback to the beach,
    almost wade into the dry, suddenlywarm air,
back to you with your beer-and-newspaper,

but it's hightide, still-calm, soggysunshine
    and this might-be-the-last because it's October;
the earth has tilted on its axis, dark
    lapping at the year, the leaves have felt it
and shivered themselves golden-and-ruddy;

so I swivel again, count-to-three and duck
    rightunder, gasping-at-shock, bob up, notdead,
lower myself again, the water coldskimming
    my back-and-shoulders with each stroke
that takes me further from changing-my-mind,

telling me this is what it means to be alive
    battling undertow current with nothing
except my own muscle and will, drenched by loss
    but never submerged, sun on face,
inhaling seaweedsmell, salt zinging lips,

every pore tingling, blinded by the brilliance of light
    frisking on water; out-of-my-depth again,
with the power in my body to choose
    to live, to do this over and over, shedding
my desk-bound, clothes-trussed self

diving in until cold has woken every millimetre
    of skin, reminded me how it's meant to feel
to be alive, alone, alive; sea-self, sunlight-self,
    swim-self; part fish, part mermaid,
part woman; part of everything.

MARCH

ha, ha, ya-di-ya,
hoikin' up the heaterin'
till all yer little froggies
start grippin' an slitherin'
broilin' up a pondstorm
spewin' out frogspawn;
an all yer soppysilly buds
simpering curtseylike
la,la,la daffydowndillys,
an all the stoopid sheepies
bleatin' well birthin'
slopperin' out their mewlin'
lambikins on the grassygreen;
an all the neverlearn peeps
optimisted, hopeblinkered
cheerfool an headsoft
let liddle chidderlins
disvest unglove castclout
slipscarf sayin' *in like a lion
out like a lamb* an me snickerin'
ha,ha, this'll learn ya
tempdrop icenose
sleetslash hailhurt
flakefall freezeball,
snowstormin' blizzardin'
hidin' up the lambkins
an the daffydillys
springclean startfresh
whitebright

EVERLOVE

everything has to be somewhere
for instance that lost earring   widowed from its partner
not in my make-up bag   not under the hairbrush
nowhere on the dressing table   not fallen down
behind or beside or into an open drawer
snuggled in the underwear not in the hoover-bag
among the dust of our discarded skin

and you must be somewhere too as physicists say
energy cannot be created or destroyed   but
you aren't in your photographs or recorded voice
inviting me to leave-a-message not in your jumper
which smells a little less of you each day
or the ashes we buried deep in case of foxes

the earring turned up   caught on a sock
and you are here   deep in the core   of me

NOW I MUST BE

both motherandfather
to myself

scatter wisdom over myownhead
like an upturned bowl of rose-petals

name myself with sprinkled water
offer pie-and-mash advice

pour out coldclean glassfuls
of forgiveness

remember to lovemyself
pridepuff at my small achievements

love mostfiercely
my flocks of imperfections

DAWN CHORUS IN AMHERST

Afterwards the lonely coo of a pigeon
and the rush-of-the-wind in the trees,
a long distant echo dyingaway
while the birds go quiet down the walk

as if they'd never sparked up a firework display
of song, erupting overoneanother in chrysanthemum
bursts of scarlet-and-bronze, comets-rising,
rockets-soaring and exploding in rainbowstars,

counterpointed Catherinewheels, waterfalls,
Romancandles, silverfountains, goldenrain,
pyrotechnics louder even than our clamours
as their siren throats swelled with air and hope

to exhale a spectacular finale, a technicolour
torrent-of-sound, reminding, insisting, in spite
of everything – there is joy in the world,
there is so much joy.

BATTING PARTNERSHIP: 34 NOT OUT
for Tim

I'm wearing ear-plugs on my sun-lounger
because the test match is blaring

from your laptop while I'm trying to read poetry,
and both of us insist on our right to the garden

because at last it's summer, and though you'd be happy
to wear head-phones if I asked, I'd still have to listen

to your school-boy cheers or furious protestations
to the umpire; so now, ear-plugged, the world

sounds underwater, like lying right back in the bath
where I can hear: my own breathing, the distant

shouts and shoe-squeaks of the basketball players
in the college gym, and faint cricketing applause

as if drifting from a far-off county or another era;
and when they stop for tea you consult me

about the pruning, and I swim up, mermaid-like
ready to exchange my voice for a dance or kiss,

and I'd like to read you the poem which prickled
my eyes with tears or the one about cricket,

which you'd catch, but Joe Root has just made 250,
so you run back to the pitch and I dive into my book

and hope this muffled afternoon is the first
of a long, hot summer where we can keep

re-crossing on the wicket, and not a warning
of the featherbed silence which will fall

when one of us is given out, and the ground
is cleared at close of play.

ALL ABOUT THE LIGHT

1

Spring Equinox

It creeps up on mossy shoes, but you're so tired
of waking to darkandcold that you don't quite believe

it'll ever come, sure the signs are false-news
sent to fool you into hope, even though they preen

in their fancy-that finery, 'hey look, we're primroses'
even when a wedding's-worth of petal confetti

flutters to your feet and the swallows write
'spring' in cursive calligraphy; reality's still the bite

of frost, the slip of ice, the murk of mornings;
till the day you wake without alarm to sunshine

lapping at your pillow, and your spiritslift to a sky
so vast that larks are sucked into it, broadcasting

height, and you rise like a bear from hibernation,
who pads to the cave-mouth, heavy with sleep,

and for one second forgets about hunger,
in the astonishment of light.

Acknowledgements

I am so grateful to the editors of the many magazines and journals in which these poems first appeared, and especially to the publishers of my previous books: Acumen Publications, Greenwich Exchange, Hearing Eye, Oversteps Books, Ward-Wood Publications and The London Magazine Editions.

I would also like to thank the friends who have helped me in the honing of these poems over the years, particularly those in the North London stanza group, and in particular those who have helped select and shape the choices for this collection: Timothy Adès, Julian Bishop, Amy Brookes, Martyn Crucefix, Stuart Handysides, Cheryl Moskowitz, Jan Stroud, Pippa Winton, Gill Wing.